Mother Nature
and Her Majestic
Kingdom,
Monthly Planner

@ Journals and Notebooks

@ Journals & Notebooks

Month: ___________________________ 2016

SUNDAY	MONDAY	TUESDAY	THURSDAY	WEDNESDAY	FRIDAY	SATURDAY

notes:

---

goals   *special projects*   *contacts*

Month: _______________________ 2016

SUNDAY	MONDAY	TUESDAY	THURSDAY	WEDNESDAY	FRIDAY	SATURDAY

notes:

____

____

____

____

____

____

goals	*special projects*	*contacts*

Month: 2016

SUNDAY	MONDAY	TUESDAY	THURSDAY	WEDNESDAY	FRIDAY	SATURDAY

notes:

goals	*special projects*	*contacts*

Month: _______________________ 2016

SUNDAY	MONDAY	TUESDAY	THURSDAY	WEDNESDAY	FRIDAY	SATURDAY

notes:

____

____

____

____

____

____

goals	*special projects*	*contacts*

Month: _______________________ 2016

SUNDAY	MONDAY	TUESDAY	THURSDAY	WEDNESDAY	FRIDAY	SATURDAY

notes:

____

____

____

____

____

____

goals	*special projects*	*contacts*

Month: *2016*

SUNDAY	MONDAY	TUESDAY	THURSDAY	WEDNESDAY	FRIDAY	SATURDAY

notes:

____

____

____

____

____

____

goals	*special projects*	*contacts*

Month: _______________________ *2016*

SUNDAY	MONDAY	TUESDAY	THURSDAY	WEDNESDAY	FRIDAY	SATURDAY

notes:

____

____

____

____

____

____

goals	*special projects*	*contacts*

Month: 2016

SUNDAY	MONDAY	TUESDAY	THURSDAY	WEDNESDAY	FRIDAY	SATURDAY

notes:

____

____

____

____

____

goals	special projects	contacts

Month: _______________________ 2016

SUNDAY	MONDAY	TUESDAY	THURSDAY	WEDNESDAY	FRIDAY	SATURDAY

notes:

____

____

____

____

____

____

goals	*special projects*	*contacts*

Month: _______________________ 2016

SUNDAY	MONDAY	TUESDAY	THURSDAY	WEDNESDAY	FRIDAY	SATURDAY

notes:

____

____

____

____

____

goals	*special projects*	*contacts*

Month: 2016

SUNDAY	MONDAY	TUESDAY	THURSDAY	WEDNESDAY	FRIDAY	SATURDAY

notes:

goals	*special projects*	*contacts*

Month: _____________ 2016

SUNDAY	MONDAY	TUESDAY	THURSDAY	WEDNESDAY	FRIDAY	SATURDAY

notes:

____

____

____

____

____

goals	*special projects*	*contacts*

Month: _______________________ 2016

SUNDAY	MONDAY	TUESDAY	THURSDAY	WEDNESDAY	FRIDAY	SATURDAY

notes:

____
____
____
____
____
____

goals	*special projects*	*contacts*

Month: *2016*

SUNDAY	MONDAY	TUESDAY	THURSDAY	WEDNESDAY	FRIDAY	SATURDAY

notes:

____

____

____

____

____

goals	*special projects*	*contacts*

Month: *2016*

SUNDAY	MONDAY	TUESDAY	THURSDAY	WEDNESDAY	FRIDAY	SATURDAY

notes:

____

____

____

____

____

goals	*special projects*	*contacts*

Month: _______________________ 2016

SUNDAY	MONDAY	TUESDAY	THURSDAY	WEDNESDAY	FRIDAY	SATURDAY

notes:

____

____

____

____

____

goals	special projects	contacts

Month: _______________________ 2016

SUNDAY	MONDAY	TUESDAY	THURSDAY	WEDNESDAY	FRIDAY	SATURDAY

notes:

____

____

____

____

____

goals	*special projects*	*contacts*

Month: _______________________ 2016

SUNDAY	MONDAY	TUESDAY	THURSDAY	WEDNESDAY	FRIDAY	SATURDAY

notes:

goals	*special projects*	*contacts*

Month: _______________________ 2016

SUNDAY	MONDAY	TUESDAY	THURSDAY	WEDNESDAY	FRIDAY	SATURDAY

notes:

____

____

____

____

____

____

goals	*special projects*	*contacts*

Month: _______________ 2016

SUNDAY	MONDAY	TUESDAY	THURSDAY	WEDNESDAY	FRIDAY	SATURDAY

notes:

____

____

____

____

____

goals	special projects	contacts

Month: _______________________ 2016

SUNDAY	MONDAY	TUESDAY	THURSDAY	WEDNESDAY	FRIDAY	SATURDAY

notes:

____

____

____

____

____

____

goals	*special projects*	*contacts*

Month: _______________ 2016

SUNDAY	MONDAY	TUESDAY	THURSDAY	WEDNESDAY	FRIDAY	SATURDAY

notes:

____

____

____

____

____

____

goals	*special projects*	*contacts*

Month: _______________________ 2016

SUNDAY	MONDAY	TUESDAY	THURSDAY	WEDNESDAY	FRIDAY	SATURDAY

notes:

____

____

____

____

____

____

goals	*special projects*	*contacts*

Month: _______________________ 2016

SUNDAY	MONDAY	TUESDAY	THURSDAY	WEDNESDAY	FRIDAY	SATURDAY

notes:

goals	*special projects*	*contacts*

Month: ______________________________ 2016

SUNDAY	MONDAY	TUESDAY	THURSDAY	WEDNESDAY	FRIDAY	SATURDAY

notes:

____

____

____

____

____

____

goals	*special projects*	*contacts*

Month: _______________________ *2016*

SUNDAY	MONDAY	TUESDAY	THURSDAY	WEDNESDAY	FRIDAY	SATURDAY

notes:

____

____

____

____

____

goals	*special projects*	*contacts*

Month: _________________ 2016

SUNDAY	MONDAY	TUESDAY	THURSDAY	WEDNESDAY	FRIDAY	SATURDAY

notes:

---

goals	*special projects*	*contacts*

Month: _______________________ 2016

SUNDAY	MONDAY	TUESDAY	THURSDAY	WEDNESDAY	FRIDAY	SATURDAY

notes:

____

____

____

____

____

goals	special projects	contacts

Month: _______________________ 2016

SUNDAY	MONDAY	TUESDAY	THURSDAY	WEDNESDAY	FRIDAY	SATURDAY

notes:

____

____

____

____

____

____

goals	*special projects*	*contacts*

Month: _______________________ 2016

SUNDAY	MONDAY	TUESDAY	THURSDAY	WEDNESDAY	FRIDAY	SATURDAY

notes:

____

____

____

____

____

goals	*special projects*	*contacts*

Month: _______________________ 2016

SUNDAY	MONDAY	TUESDAY	THURSDAY	WEDNESDAY	FRIDAY	SATURDAY

notes:

____

____

____

____

____

goals	*special projects*	*contacts*

Month: _________________________ 2016

SUNDAY	MONDAY	TUESDAY	THURSDAY	WEDNESDAY	FRIDAY	SATURDAY

notes:

goals	*special projects*	*contacts*

Month: _______________________ 2016

SUNDAY	MONDAY	TUESDAY	THURSDAY	WEDNESDAY	FRIDAY	SATURDAY

notes:

____

____

____

____

____

____

goals	*special projects*	*contacts*

Month: _______________________ 2016

SUNDAY	MONDAY	TUESDAY	THURSDAY	WEDNESDAY	FRIDAY	SATURDAY

notes:

____

____

____

____

____

____

goals	*special projects*	*contacts*

Month: 2016

SUNDAY	MONDAY	TUESDAY	THURSDAY	WEDNESDAY	FRIDAY	SATURDAY

notes:

____

____

____

____

____

____

goals	*special projects*	*contacts*

Month: ____________________ *2016*

SUNDAY	MONDAY	TUESDAY	THURSDAY	WEDNESDAY	FRIDAY	SATURDAY

notes:

____

____

____

____

____

goals	*special projects*	*contacts*

Month: _______________________________   2016

SUNDAY	MONDAY	TUESDAY	THURSDAY	WEDNESDAY	FRIDAY	SATURDAY

notes:

____

goals	*special projects*	*contacts*

Month: ____________________ 2016

SUNDAY	MONDAY	TUESDAY	THURSDAY	WEDNESDAY	FRIDAY	SATURDAY

notes:

____
____
____
____
____
____

goals	*special projects*	*contacts*

Month: _______________________ 2016

SUNDAY	MONDAY	TUESDAY	THURSDAY	WEDNESDAY	FRIDAY	SATURDAY

notes:

____
____
____
____
____

goals	*special projects*	*contacts*

Month: _______________________ 2016

SUNDAY	MONDAY	TUESDAY	THURSDAY	WEDNESDAY	FRIDAY	SATURDAY

notes:

____

____

____

____

____

goals	*special projects*	*contacts*

Month: _______________________ 2016

SUNDAY	MONDAY	TUESDAY	THURSDAY	WEDNESDAY	FRIDAY	SATURDAY

notes:

____

____

____

____

____

goals	*special projects*	*contacts*

Month: _________________________ 2016

SUNDAY	MONDAY	TUESDAY	THURSDAY	WEDNESDAY	FRIDAY	SATURDAY

notes:

____

____

____

____

____

____

goals	*special projects*	*contacts*

Month: _______________ 2016

SUNDAY	MONDAY	TUESDAY	THURSDAY	WEDNESDAY	FRIDAY	SATURDAY

notes:

____

____

____

____

____

goals	*special projects*	*contacts*

Month: _______________________________ 2016

SUNDAY	MONDAY	TUESDAY	THURSDAY	WEDNESDAY	FRIDAY	SATURDAY

notes:

goals	special projects	contacts

Month: _______________________ 2016

SUNDAY	MONDAY	TUESDAY	THURSDAY	WEDNESDAY	FRIDAY	SATURDAY

notes:

____

____

____

____

____

____

goals	*special projects*	*contacts*

Month: _______________ 2016

SUNDAY	MONDAY	TUESDAY	THURSDAY	WEDNESDAY	FRIDAY	SATURDAY

notes:

____

____

____

____

____

goals	*special projects*	*contacts*

Month: _______________ 2016

SUNDAY	MONDAY	TUESDAY	THURSDAY	WEDNESDAY	FRIDAY	SATURDAY

notes:

____

____

____

____

____

goals	*special projects*	*contacts*

Month: 2016

SUNDAY	MONDAY	TUESDAY	THURSDAY	WEDNESDAY	FRIDAY	SATURDAY

notes:

____

____

____

____

____

____

goals	*special projects*	*contacts*

Month: _______________________ 2016

SUNDAY	MONDAY	TUESDAY	THURSDAY	WEDNESDAY	FRIDAY	SATURDAY

notes:

____

____

____

____

____

____

goals	*special projects*	*contacts*

Month: _________________________ 2016

SUNDAY	MONDAY	TUESDAY	THURSDAY	WEDNESDAY	FRIDAY	SATURDAY

notes:

____

____

____

____

____

____

goals	*special projects*	*contacts*

Month: _____________________ 2016

SUNDAY	MONDAY	TUESDAY	THURSDAY	WEDNESDAY	FRIDAY	SATURDAY

notes:

____

____

____

____

____

____

goals	*special projects*	*contacts*

Month: _________________________ 2016

SUNDAY	MONDAY	TUESDAY	THURSDAY	WEDNESDAY	FRIDAY	SATURDAY

notes:

____

____

____

____

____

goals	*special projects*	*contacts*

Month: ____ 2016

SUNDAY	MONDAY	TUESDAY	THURSDAY	WEDNESDAY	FRIDAY	SATURDAY

notes:

____

____

____

____

____

____

goals	*special projects*	*contacts*

Month: _______________________ 2016

SUNDAY	MONDAY	TUESDAY	THURSDAY	WEDNESDAY	FRIDAY	SATURDAY

notes:

____

____

____

____

____

goals	*special projects*	*contacts*

Month: _____ 2016

SUNDAY	MONDAY	TUESDAY	THURSDAY	WEDNESDAY	FRIDAY	SATURDAY

notes:

____

____

____

____

____

____

goals	*special projects*	*contacts*

Month: 2016

SUNDAY	MONDAY	TUESDAY	THURSDAY	WEDNESDAY	FRIDAY	SATURDAY

notes:

____

____

____

____

____

goals	*special projects*	*contacts*

Month: ____________________ 2016

SUNDAY	MONDAY	TUESDAY	THURSDAY	WEDNESDAY	FRIDAY	SATURDAY

notes:

____

____

____

____

____

goals	*special projects*	*contacts*

Month: _______________________ 2016

SUNDAY	MONDAY	TUESDAY	THURSDAY	WEDNESDAY	FRIDAY	SATURDAY

notes:

____

____

____

____

____

____

goals	*special projects*	*contacts*

Month: 2016

SUNDAY	MONDAY	TUESDAY	THURSDAY	WEDNESDAY	FRIDAY	SATURDAY

notes:

____

____

____

____

____

____

goals	*special projects*	*contacts*

Month: _____________________ 2016

SUNDAY	MONDAY	TUESDAY	THURSDAY	WEDNESDAY	FRIDAY	SATURDAY

notes:

____

____

____

____

____

goals	*special projects*	*contacts*

Month: ___________________________ 2016

SUNDAY	MONDAY	TUESDAY	THURSDAY	WEDNESDAY	FRIDAY	SATURDAY

notes:

____

____

____

____

____

____

goals	*special projects*	*contacts*

Month: _______________________ 2016

SUNDAY	MONDAY	TUESDAY	THURSDAY	WEDNESDAY	FRIDAY	SATURDAY

notes:

goals | *special projects* | *contacts*

Month: _______________ 2016

SUNDAY	MONDAY	TUESDAY	THURSDAY	WEDNESDAY	FRIDAY	SATURDAY

notes:

____

____

____

____

____

goals	*special projects*	*contacts*

Month: ________________________ 2016

SUNDAY	MONDAY	TUESDAY	THURSDAY	WEDNESDAY	FRIDAY	SATURDAY

notes:

____

____

____

____

____

goals	*special projects*	*contacts*

Month: 2016

SUNDAY	MONDAY	TUESDAY	THURSDAY	WEDNESDAY	FRIDAY	SATURDAY

notes:

____

____

____

____

____

goals	*special projects*	*contacts*

Month: _______________________ 2016

SUNDAY	MONDAY	TUESDAY	THURSDAY	WEDNESDAY	FRIDAY	SATURDAY

notes:

____

____

____

____

____

____

goals	*special projects*	*contacts*

Month: *2016*

SUNDAY	MONDAY	TUESDAY	THURSDAY	WEDNESDAY	FRIDAY	SATURDAY

notes:

goals	*special projects*	*contacts*

Month: ___________________ 2016

SUNDAY	MONDAY	TUESDAY	THURSDAY	WEDNESDAY	FRIDAY	SATURDAY

notes:

____

____

____

____

____

goals	*special projects*	*contacts*

Month: _______________ 2016

SUNDAY	MONDAY	TUESDAY	THURSDAY	WEDNESDAY	FRIDAY	SATURDAY

notes:

goals | *special projects* | *contacts*

Month: _______________________ 2016

SUNDAY	MONDAY	TUESDAY	THURSDAY	WEDNESDAY	FRIDAY	SATURDAY

notes:

____

____

____

____

____

goals	*special projects*	*contacts*

Month: _______________ 2016

SUNDAY	MONDAY	TUESDAY	THURSDAY	WEDNESDAY	FRIDAY	SATURDAY

notes:

____
____
____
____
____

goals	*special projects*	*contacts*

Month: *2016*

SUNDAY	MONDAY	TUESDAY	THURSDAY	WEDNESDAY	FRIDAY	SATURDAY

notes:

____

____

____

____

____

____

goals	*special projects*	*contacts*

Month: _______________________ 2016

SUNDAY	MONDAY	TUESDAY	THURSDAY	WEDNESDAY	FRIDAY	SATURDAY

notes:

____

____

____

____

____

goals	*special projects*	*contacts*

Month: ___________________________ 2016

SUNDAY	MONDAY	TUESDAY	THURSDAY	WEDNESDAY	FRIDAY	SATURDAY

notes:

____

____

____

____

____

____

goals	*special projects*	*contacts*

Month: 2016

SUNDAY	MONDAY	TUESDAY	THURSDAY	WEDNESDAY	FRIDAY	SATURDAY

notes:

____

____

____

____

____

____

goals	*special projects*	*contacts*

Month: *2016*

SUNDAY	MONDAY	TUESDAY	THURSDAY	WEDNESDAY	FRIDAY	SATURDAY

notes:

____

____

____

____

____

goals	*special projects*	*contacts*

Month: __________________ 2016

SUNDAY	MONDAY	TUESDAY	THURSDAY	WEDNESDAY	FRIDAY	SATURDAY

notes:

goals | *special projects* | *contacts*

Month: _______________________________ 2016

SUNDAY	MONDAY	TUESDAY	THURSDAY	WEDNESDAY	FRIDAY	SATURDAY

notes:

____

____

____

____

____

____

goals	*special projects*	*contacts*

Month: *2016*

SUNDAY	MONDAY	TUESDAY	THURSDAY	WEDNESDAY	FRIDAY	SATURDAY

notes:

____

____

____

____

____

____

goals	*special projects*	*contacts*

Month: 2016

SUNDAY	MONDAY	TUESDAY	THURSDAY	WEDNESDAY	FRIDAY	SATURDAY

notes:

____

____

____

____

____

goals	*special projects*	*contacts*

Month: _______________________ 2016

SUNDAY	MONDAY	TUESDAY	THURSDAY	WEDNESDAY	FRIDAY	SATURDAY

notes:

____

____

____

____

____

goals	*special projects*	*contacts*

Month: ___________________ *2016*

SUNDAY	MONDAY	TUESDAY	THURSDAY	WEDNESDAY	FRIDAY	SATURDAY

notes:

____

____

____

____

____

____

goals	*special projects*	*contacts*

Month: ________________________ *2016*

SUNDAY	MONDAY	TUESDAY	THURSDAY	WEDNESDAY	FRIDAY	SATURDAY

notes:

____
____
____
____
____
____

goals	*special projects*	*contacts*

Month: _______________________ *2016*

SUNDAY	MONDAY	TUESDAY	THURSDAY	WEDNESDAY	FRIDAY	SATURDAY

notes:

____

____

____

____

____

goals	*special projects*	*contacts*

Month: 2016

SUNDAY	MONDAY	TUESDAY	THURSDAY	WEDNESDAY	FRIDAY	SATURDAY

notes:

____

____

____

____

____

____

goals	*special projects*	*contacts*

Month: ___________________ 2016

SUNDAY	MONDAY	TUESDAY	THURSDAY	WEDNESDAY	FRIDAY	SATURDAY

notes:

____

____

____

____

____

goals	*special projects*	*contacts*

Month: _______________________ 2016

SUNDAY	MONDAY	TUESDAY	THURSDAY	WEDNESDAY	FRIDAY	SATURDAY

notes:

____

____

____

____

____

goals	*special projects*	*contacts*

Month: _______________________ 2016

SUNDAY	MONDAY	TUESDAY	THURSDAY	WEDNESDAY	FRIDAY	SATURDAY

notes:

____

____

____

____

____

goals	special projects	contacts

Month: ________________ *2016*

SUNDAY	MONDAY	TUESDAY	THURSDAY	WEDNESDAY	FRIDAY	SATURDAY

notes:

____

____

____

____

____

goals	*special projects*	*contacts*

Month: _________________________ 2016

SUNDAY	MONDAY	TUESDAY	THURSDAY	WEDNESDAY	FRIDAY	SATURDAY

notes:

____

____

____

____

____

____

goals	*special projects*	*contacts*

Month: _______________ 2016

SUNDAY	MONDAY	TUESDAY	THURSDAY	WEDNESDAY	FRIDAY	SATURDAY

notes:

____

____

____

____

____

____

goals	*special projects*	*contacts*

Month: _______________________ 2016

SUNDAY	MONDAY	TUESDAY	THURSDAY	WEDNESDAY	FRIDAY	SATURDAY

notes:

____

____

____

____

____

____

goals	*special projects*	*contacts*

Month: __________________________ 2016

SUNDAY	MONDAY	TUESDAY	THURSDAY	WEDNESDAY	FRIDAY	SATURDAY

notes:

____

____

____

____

____

____

goals	*special projects*	*contacts*

Month: _______________________ 2016

SUNDAY	MONDAY	TUESDAY	THURSDAY	WEDNESDAY	FRIDAY	SATURDAY

notes:

____

____

____

____

____

goals	*special projects*	*contacts*

Month: _______________________________ 2016

SUNDAY	MONDAY	TUESDAY	THURSDAY	WEDNESDAY	FRIDAY	SATURDAY

notes:

____

____

____

____

____

____

goals	*special projects*	*contacts*

Month: _______________________________ *2016*

SUNDAY	MONDAY	TUESDAY	THURSDAY	WEDNESDAY	FRIDAY	SATURDAY

notes:

____

____

____

____

____

____

goals	*special projects*	*contacts*

Month: 2016

SUNDAY	MONDAY	TUESDAY	THURSDAY	WEDNESDAY	FRIDAY	SATURDAY

notes:

____

____

____

____

____

goals	*special projects*	*contacts*

Month: _______________________ *2016*

SUNDAY	MONDAY	TUESDAY	THURSDAY	WEDNESDAY	FRIDAY	SATURDAY

notes:

____

____

____

____

____

goals	*special projects*	*contacts*

Month: 2016

SUNDAY	MONDAY	TUESDAY	THURSDAY	WEDNESDAY	FRIDAY	SATURDAY

notes:

____

____

____

____

____

____

goals	*special projects*	*contacts*

Month: _______________________ 2016

SUNDAY	MONDAY	TUESDAY	THURSDAY	WEDNESDAY	FRIDAY	SATURDAY

notes:

____

____

____

____

____

goals	special projects	contacts

Month: _______________________ 2016

SUNDAY	MONDAY	TUESDAY	THURSDAY	WEDNESDAY	FRIDAY	SATURDAY

notes:

____
____
____
____
____
____

goals	*special projects*	*contacts*

Month: _______________ 2016

SUNDAY	MONDAY	TUESDAY	THURSDAY	WEDNESDAY	FRIDAY	SATURDAY

notes:

____

____

____

____

____

goals	*special projects*	*contacts*

Month: _______________________ 2016

SUNDAY	MONDAY	TUESDAY	THURSDAY	WEDNESDAY	FRIDAY	SATURDAY

notes:

____
____
____
____
____
____

goals	*special projects*	*contacts*

Month: 2016

SUNDAY	MONDAY	TUESDAY	THURSDAY	WEDNESDAY	FRIDAY	SATURDAY

notes:

____

____

____

____

____

goals	*special projects*	*contacts*